40 ESSENTIAL SOCCER STRETCHES

Warm-up and Cool-down with Yoga

Fiona Leard

Foreword by John Aloisi

The ideas and suggestions in this manual are the opinions of the author only. If you are not trained in the areas of fitness and yoga, it is advisable to consult a qualified practitioner before beginning any new exercise technique.

The author makes no warranty of any kind to the content of this book regarding specific fitness for any particular purpose. The reader assumes all liability for the use of the exercises and stretches provided. The author is not responsible to any person or entity for errors contained in this book or incidental, or consequential, damage caused, or alleged to be caused, directly or indirectly by the information.

Children under the age of 16 should be closely supervised by an adult or qualified practitioner when undertaking the programs in this book.

CONTENTS

Foreword vii

Preface ix

Chapter 1: Using Yoga to Warm-up and Cool-down 1

Chapter 2: Poses to Warm-up With 5

Chapter 3: Cool-down Stretches 31

About The Author 55

About The Models 57

FOREWORD
by John Aloisi

I began practicing yoga when I was 32-years-old. I started because my knees were shot and the cartilage was worn out. I didn't feel as though I was ready to retire from professional football, so I was willing to try anything to prolong my career. Like every professional athlete, I started to ask myself what could be out there that would help me maintain my body at a level that would allow me to continue to compete? And one answer kept coming up for me. It was yoga.

I wondered what style of yoga would best suit me as a soccer player and I knew there was one guy who had done as much homework on the subject as I had and suffered similar injuries during his playing career. He was Tony Popovic, an ex-teammate and then one of my coaches at Sydney Football Club. He practiced yoga with Fiona to maintain his body for competition during his last season as a professional player and he introduced me to her.

I have to admit I was a bit sceptical but I had nothing to lose because my body felt terrible. I struggled at first. I couldn't get into the positions because I was so stiff, but I persisted. After one month I noticed my muscles releasing. My back wasn't hurting anymore and there was less pressure on my knees. I realised that through yoga I had gained full extension in my left knee for the first time in about three years. The best thing, however, was that my head was also clear and the usual stresses that come along with playing professional football weren't getting to me anymore.

The previous year I had been plagued by injury and performed poorly, so there was a lot of pressure on me to stay fit and play well. I worked privately with Fiona and the club also integrated yoga into our training schedule. The players loved it and the proof was there for all to see. We won the minor premiership and the grand final that year. Not only was I leading goal scorer, but I reached double figures, the first player to achieve that at Sydney Football Club.

I moved to Melbourne Heart Football Club the following season where we also used yoga in our training program. Yoga helped me play a little longer at a high level at the end of my playing career. It's made me more flexible and a lot stronger through the core and hips and it's improved my balance. Now that I've retired from playing, yoga is still an important part of my life.

John Aloisi was an integral member of the Australian 'Socceroos' National Team and a highly celebrated player. His professional career has spanned 20 seasons across the United Kingdom, Europe and Australia. He's a great ambassador for the sport in Australia and now continues his career as a Manager.

PREFACE

Stretching for soccer is not a new concept and a thorough warm-up and cool-down is essential in all training sessions and games to enhance physical and mental performance and reduce the risk of injury. Due to the repetitive nature of the movements of the back, hips and legs in soccer, it's important to release all major joints and muscle groups in the feet, legs, hips and torso before and after the game to prevent muscle imbalances that can lead to poor performance.

Yoga is a fantastic complement to your training and competition schedule to help maintain your body for sport. The warm-up and cool-down routines in this book have been inspired by yoga postures that not only improve flexibility, but also enhance circulation, increase mobility, maintain joint health, balance your nervous system, help you breathe better and relax your mind. Yoga will heat your body and prepare the muscles and joints for more intense activity and it will aid recovery and regeneration when practiced at the end of a session. The stretching sequences in this book have been adapted from *The Yoga Edge: Techniques to Maximize Your Soccer Game* and are a great way to boost your performance. The programs should be used three to four times a week, but can be used daily when training and playing regularly. These are the yoga programs I provide soccer players with to add to their daily routine to take care of their bodies during pre-season and competition.

In this easy-to-use book, I will explain the advantages of using yoga with your training program:

Chapter 1 explains the benefits of using yoga to stretch and why your warm-up and cool-down are fundamental to maintaining your body in order to prevent injury and improve performance on the pitch.

Chapter 2 contains a 10 minute dynamic sequence designed to prepare the footballer's body for warm-up prior to training or a game. It ensures you move your ankles, knees, hips and spine through a full range of movement and provides gentle dynamic stretching for all the major muscles groups recruited when playing football.

Chapter 3 illustrates a 10 to 15 minute program for use at the end of your session or game to maintain flexibility and restore balance to your muscular system and joints. It assists with the recovery process and involves more restful poses, held for at least one to three minutes each. This helps to release tension, improve blood flow to the muscles and free connective tissue to restore joint health.

Using these routines is a great way to incorporate some of the benefits of yoga into your training regime and your life. Both these programs are simple to follow and this book contains the basic instructions required to perform each pose correctly, the breathing methods used and a page with the poses in sequence. The major muscles and joints utilised are identified along with variations to modify the stretches if required. The warm-up and cool-down routines are suitable for players of all ages and fitness levels. They have been designed to help you get the most out of your body and sustain a long and injury free career no matter what level you play at.

CHAPTER 1

Using Yoga to Warm-up and Cool-down

The importance of a proper warm-up and cool-down before and after your training sessions and games is well-known. All sessions should be preceded by a good warm-up that includes general large muscle movements, dynamic stretching and soccer specific drills. The purpose of the warm-up is to increase muscle temperature, promote blood flow and prepare the body's systems for intense physical activity. A thorough stretching routine should be included in the warm-up as tight muscles can weaken, cramp or even tear. Reduced mobility of the hips can cause back or knee pain and tight calf muscles or Achilles tendons can increase stress on the knee joints or reduce ankle joint stability. A dynamic yoga sequence is very useful prior to your warm-up session to prepare your mind and body adequately for exercise and enhance your performance on the pitch.

Every training session and game you play should finish with a cool-down session. This generally involves low intensity activity and static stretching to return the body to its natural resting state. This includes lowering the heart rate, blood pressure and breathing rate, eliminating waste products from the tissues, cooling the body and switching on the recovery process. The right type of yoga used during the cool-down will allow the body to relax and begin the rejuvenation process more rapidly than a few quick stretches.

The benefits of using yoga over static stretching in your warm-up and cool-down are numerous. Yoga is a union of physical postures, breathing, focus, concentration and relaxation that brings about a wide range of physical and psychological benefits. The yoga advantage is gained as a result of gentle controlled movements, combined with breathing and awareness, that nourish your muscles, joints and organs and strengthen your mind, making yoga a great complement to any sporting activity.

THE BENEFITS OF YOGA IN WARM-UP

By including the warm-up yoga sequence regularly before your training you will maintain the health of your body's muscles, joints, organs and tissues. You will also prepare yourself physically and mentally to perform at your best every time you run onto the pitch.

MOBILITY increases throughout your entire body and muscular tension is released from your legs, hips and torso by moving through a range of dynamic stretches that increase circulation and heat your body. Joints begin to warm as you increase core temperature and circulate synovial fluid and joint discomfort is reduced as muscle tension dissolves, promoting good alignment and posture.

ENERGY increases as your nervous system is activated by dynamic postures that prepare you for more intense activity by increasing circulation, breathing and metabolism.

OXYGEN levels rise in your body as you regulate your breathing throughout the sequence and include partial inversions that allow blood to saturate your lung tissue and transfer oxygen to your bloodstream and muscle cells.

FOCUS is enhanced for training and competition by creating a moving meditation through controlled breathing and an awareness of the sensations in your body as you flow through the sequence.

THE BENEFITS OF YOGA IN COOL-DOWN

Yin-inspired yoga is ideal after training and playing to promote regeneration, as you recover faster when you're relaxed. These pose are combined with slow deep breathing, performed mostly seated and lying, and are held for a longer period of time.

RECOVERY is improved as the nervous system is calmed and you relax when practicing more restful poses. Adrenaline and cortisol levels decrease and circulation and oxygenation to all tissues in the body increases to boost the rejuvenation process.

DIGESTION is promoted following training through relaxation of the nervous system and increased blood flow to the abdominal organs and the digestive tract. This is important so that the nutrients you take in following training can be digested and absorbed efficiently.

FLEXIBILITY of muscles and deeper layers of connective tissue is restored as tension is released from the body and mind with gentle stretches held for a longer duration. Joints are also conditioned as connective tissue relaxes and restores a healthy range of movement.

RISK OF INJURY IS REDUCED as the body returns to its natural resting state and muscles and connective tissue are released, decreasing muscular imbalances that can lead to soft tissue injury further down the track.

CHAPTER 2

Poses to Warm-up With

Dynamic yoga-inspired movements can be incorporated into your warm-up routine to heat your muscles and joints, increase circulation and improve mobility throughout your entire body, preparing you physically and mentally for training and competition. The focus of this program is moving your ankles, knees, hips and spine through a full range of motion and mobilising the body from head to toe. Regulated breathing is incorporated to increase oxygen levels in the body and to encourage the mind to focus and concentrate. This gentle, yet dynamic, stretching routine requires 10 minutes to perform and is good preparation for more ballistic stretching and the rest of your football specific activities. Use this sequence at home every morning or at the training ground before you begin your warm-up routine.

TIPS FOR DYNAMIC WARM-UP

BREATHING

Breathe through your nose to maintain focus and body awareness and continue to heat your body. Use your throat muscles to initiate your inhale and exhale rather than your nostrils as it lengthens the time you take to breathe in and out. This will slow your breathing rate, which balances your nervous system (and helps manage stress), oxygenates your cells and creates a sound that you can listen to so you become more focused. It's important that you don't hold your breath throughout the poses as the benefits of the breathing will be lost.

TIMING

Flow rhythmically from one pose to the next using the sound of your breath to regulate the speed of your movement. You can increase the number of repetitions for each pose if you feel you need more time for your muscles to release. Hold stretches for a maximum of 10 seconds to avoid the stretches becoming static and relaxing for the body.

INTENSITY

Move within a comfortable range for you and increase the movements gradually as your body begins to warm and your muscles and joints become free.

SAFETY

Honour your body and move only through a range that is appropriate for your physical condition. Maintain good posture and engage your core muscles by gently drawing in the point slightly below your belly button. If your muscles are sore, stretch gently. If you have an injury, seek medical clearance prior to stretching and if any stretch causes you pain (not stretching discomfort), avoid that movement for the time being and seek advice from a qualified practitioner if necessary.

WARM-UP

1. Standing Side Bend

Three to five times each side

Mobilises the spine.
Stretches the sides of the abdominal, hip and thigh muscles.
Expands the ribcage to allow easier breathing.

1a: Standing Side Bend – start   1b: Standing Side Bend

- Stand with your feet together.
- Interlace your hands above your head, with palms facing up (1a).
- Inhale and press down through both feet. Exhale to a side bend (1b) until you feel a stretch in the side of your torso (keep your legs and core muscles strong and bend from your upper spine).
- Inhale as you move back to the centre and exhale to the other side.

2. Forward Fold

Hold for five to ten seconds
Stretches the calf muscles, hamstrings and lower back muscles. Releases the neck.

2: Forward Fold

- Stand with your feet hip-width apart and bend your knees.
- As you exhale, tighten your core muscles and fold forward from the hips. Avoid bending from your lower back.
- Hold your elbows, relax your face and neck and let your head hang.
- Press both feet into the ground and sway your torso gently from side to side to release your lower back muscles. You can also alternate bending one leg and straightening the other to release your hamstrings more.
- Focus on lengthening the backs of your legs by pressing your heels down and your hips up at the same time. This will maintain the stretch in your hamstrings and calf muscles.
- Gently nod your head and turn it side to side five times in each direction to release your neck muscles.
- Keep breathing steadily.

3. Downward-Facing Dog

Hold for five to ten seconds

Stretches the calf muscles, the arches of the feet, hamstrings and gluteal muscles.
Mobilises the ankle joints.
Expands the ribcage for easier breathing.
Increases blood flow to the lungs and oxygen levels in the body.

3a: Downward-Facing Dog

- Place your hands shoulder-width apart on the ground and press your palms down firmly.
- Step your feet back as far as you can, place them parallel, bend your knees, pull your abdominals in and lift your hips to the sky to stretch your hamstrings.

- Press down through the balls of your feet and lower your heels towards the ground to stretch your calf muscles.
- Keep pressing firmly into your palms, drawing the bottom tips of your shoulder blades into your back. Breathe into your ribcage, expanding it sideways.
- To focus more on stretching your calf muscles walk your heels down one at a time towards the ground. Repeat five times on each side.

3b: Calf Stretch

- Press one heel down at a time and hold for five seconds for a stronger calf stretch (3b).
- Hold one heel down and circle the opposite ankle five times in each direction to mobilise your ankle joints.
- Repeat with the other leg.

4. Upward-Facing Dog

Hold for five seconds

Extends the spine.
Opens the chest for better breathing.

4: Upward-Facing Dog

- From Downward-Facing Dog come into a plank position with your shoulders over your wrists and body in a straight line. Either lower your body halfway down (like a push-up), or lie on the ground and, with your hands beside your ribcage, press into your palms and lift your chest.
- If your lower back feels comfortable extend your arms to Upward-Facing Dog, otherwise lift only to the height where your lower back is comfortable.
- Keep your core muscles engaged, your shoulders back and press the tops of your feet into the ground. Pull your chest forward to maximise the stretch in the front of your body.
- Breathe into the front and sides of your ribcage.

5. Downward-Facing Dog

Hold for five seconds

Stretches the calf muscles, the arches of the feet, hamstrings and gluteal muscles.
Expands the ribcage.
Increases blood flow to the lungs and oxygen levels in the body.

5: Downward-Facing Dog

- From Cobra or Upward-Facing Dog, press your hands into the ground and lift your hips to Downward-Facing Dog.
- Take some deep breaths, drop both heels towards the ground and press your hips up to the sky.

Repeat **Plank, Upward-Facing Dog** and **Downward-Facing Dog** five times with one breath in each position.

6. Crescent Lunge

Hold for one to three breaths

Awakens hip, knee and ankle stabilising muscles.
Improves balance.
Stretches the hip flexors of the back leg.

6: Crescent Lunge

- From Downward-Facing Dog, step your right foot forward and place it inside your right hand.
- As you inhale, press down into your front foot, lift your torso and raise your arms above your head.
- Bend your front knee to 90 degrees, keeping toes, knee and hip aligned and pointing straight ahead. You will feel your thigh, hamstrings and gluteal muscles activate.
- Press down through the ball of your back foot and straighten your back leg to stretch your hip flexors.
- Engage your core to keep your hips level.
- Focus on pulling your feet towards the centre of your mat to maintain alignment and stability.

7. Warrior II

Hold for one to three breaths
Stretches the groin muscles and opens the hips.

7: Warrior II

- From Crescent Lunge, as you exhale, turn your back heel flat and rotate your hips and shoulders to face the side. Press down through the outside edge of your back foot and keep your front knee stacked above your ankle. Your heels should be in line.
- Draw your front ribs into your body to engage your core.
- Arms should be at shoulder height, with shoulders relaxed.
- Focus on drawing your heels towards each other and your thighbones into your hip sockets.
- To increase the stretch on your groin muscles lunge deeper.

8. Reverse Warrior

Hold for one to three breaths
Stretches the groin muscles and side of the torso
Opens the ribcage.

8: Reverse Warrior

- From Warrior II, reach your front hand to the sky as you inhale.
- Keep your core muscles engaged and both sides of your torso lengthened.
- Breathe into the sides of your ribcage.
- To release, place both hands back to the ground as you exhale and move to low push-up position, take a breath in as you move to Upward-Facing Dog (4) and breathe out to Downward-Facing Dog (5).
- Repeat Crescent Lunge, Warrior II and Reverse Warrior on the left leg.

Repeat three times each side **Crescent Lunge**, **Warrior II**, **Reverse Warrior**, **Upward-Facing Dog** and **Downward-Facing Dog** with one breath in each pose.

9. Rocking Lunge

Five to ten times

Stretches the hip flexors, hamstrings and gluteal muscles. Mobilises the hip and knee joints.

9a: Low Lunge

9b: Half Splits

- From Downward-Facing Dog, step one foot forward in line with your hands.
- Drop your back knee to the ground and place your hands on your front thigh.
- As you breathe in, lower your hips forward to Low Lunge and lift your chest to stretch the front of your back hip (9a).
- As you exhale, rock your hips back and drop your forehead towards your shin for Half Splits to stretch your gluteals and hamstrings (9b).
- You can flex your front foot towards your shin for a stronger hamstring and calf stretch.
- Maintain the contraction of your core muscles throughout this exercise.

10. Quad Lunge

Hold for ten seconds
Stretches the quadriceps and hip flexor muscles.

10a: Quad Lunge   10b: Lying Quad Stretch

- From Low Lunge (9a), pick up your back foot with the hand on the same side of your body (10a). For a more intense quad stretch hold your ankle and flex your foot. You can hold with two hands if you have the mobility.
- Keep your core muscles engaged as you draw your back heel towards your hip to increase the stretch in your quadriceps and hip flexors.
- Breathe steadily as you hold this position.
- If your thigh muscles are tight and you can't reach your back foot you can lie face down to do this (10b).

11. Half Splits

Hold for ten seconds

Releases the hamstrings, gluteals and calf muscles.

11: Half Splits

- From Low Lunge, move your hips over your back knee until you feel a stretch in your hamstrings.
- Drop your forehead towards your front shin. Bend your front knee if your hamstrings are tight.
- Pull your front toes back towards your face to increase the stretch in your calf muscles.
- Breathe slowly as you hold here.

Repeat **Rocking Lunge, Quad Lunge** and **Half Splits** on the other side.

12. Side-Rocking Lunge

Five to ten times on each side

Stretches the groin, inner hamstrings and the front of the shins. Mobilises the lower back, hips, knees and ankles.

12: Side-Rocking Lunge

- From Low Lunge, spin your body around to the side so you are in a wide-leg straddle with your hands on the ground and feet parallel.
- Bend your knees if your hamstrings and groin muscles are tight.
- Bend one leg and straighten the other until you feel your inner thighs stretching. Rock gently from side to side.
- Keep your feet flat on the ground and parallel to stretch your shin muscles.
- Inhale as you move through the centre and exhale into the side lunge.

13. Side Lunge

Hold for five to ten seconds
Stretches the long inner thigh muscles, hamstrings and calves.

13: Side Lunge

- From wide-leg straddle, turn your toes out and squat down onto one leg.
- Keep your hands on the inside of your bent leg.
- If the stretch in your groin or hamstring muscles is too strong, rest your elbows on your bent leg and lunge halfway down.

14. Squat

Hold five to ten seconds

Stretches the arches of the feet and toes.
Stretches the short groin muscles.
Releases the hip joints and lower back.

14a: Squat   14b: Squat with prayer hands

- From wide-leg straddle place your heels together with your toes pointing out.
- Lift your heels and squat your hips as close to the ground as possible.
- Keep your fingers on the ground shoulder-width apart for support and rise as far onto your toes as you can to stretch your feet.
- Then press your elbows into the insides of your knees and lean forward. Hold this position for five to ten seconds.
- To finish, place your palms together in prayer (14b) with your elbows on the insides of your thighs, lift your chest and gently rotate your hips for another five to ten seconds.
- Release slowly from this pose, by placing your hands on the ground, draw your knees together and then sit down.

15. Seated Hip Roll

Five to ten times on each side
Stretches the internal and external rotator muscles of the hip joint. Rotates and mobilises the lower back.

15: Seated Hip Roll

- Sit down and rest back on your hands, with your knees bent to 90 degrees and feet wider than your hips.
- Roll your knees from side to side, dropping them as close to the ground as possible to release tension in your hip joints and lower back.
- Keep your core muscles engaged.
- Inhale as you move through the centre and exhale into the hip roll.

16. Seated Half Pigeon

Hold for five to ten seconds
Stretches the gluteal and groin muscles.

16: Seated Half Pigeon

- From your seated position, take your hands behind you and bend your knees. Place one ankle over the thigh of your opposite leg and flex your foot.
- Take a deep breath in and straighten your spine; then slowly breathe out as you lift your chest towards your shin and you feel a stretch in the gluteal muscles of your crossed leg.
- Gently roll your knees from side to side for a few breaths to release your hips.
- Repeat on the other leg.

17. Lying Hip Roll

Five to ten on each side
Gently mobilises the spine and hips.

17a: Lying Hip Roll – feet wide   17b: Lying Hip Roll – feet together

- Lie on your back and bend your knees to 90 degrees with your feet wider than your hips.
- Roll your knees from side to side as you inhale and exhale, allowing them to drop as close to the ground as possible.
- Turn your head in the opposite direction to your knees to stretch your neck.
- Perform five to ten hip rolls with your feet slightly wider than your hips to focus on internal and external hip rotation.
- Perform five to ten hip rolls with your feet together, bringing more focus to the muscles and joints in your lower back.

18. Supine Straight-Leg Rolls

Five to ten on each side
Stretches the muscles of the outer thigh, hip and torso.
Mobilises the spine in rotation.

18a: Supine Straight-Leg Roll   18b: Supine Revolving Leg – hold

- Lie on your back with your arms at 90 degrees to your body, palms facing up or down, legs straight and feet hip-width apart.
- Press one heel into the ground and roll the other leg across your body towards your opposite hand (18a) as you exhale. Move within the range that provides a stretch in your back and outer thigh on each side.
- Keep your core muscles engaged and your shoulders on the ground.
- To finish, hold the end position for five to ten seconds on each side with your opposite hand supporting your leg (18b).

19. Prone Revolving Leg Rolls

Five to ten on each side
Stretches rotational muscles on the front of the torso, the chest and the front of the shoulders.
Mobilises the spine in rotation.

19: Prone Revolving Leg Rolls

- Lie face down with your arms at 90 degrees to your body, palms down and feet hip-width apart.
- Press both palms into the ground. Keep your chin tucked in towards your chest and your core muscles tight.
- Bend one leg and lift it over behind your body until your foot touches the ground (if your torso and hips are tight, your foot may not touch). Only move to the point in which you feel a moderate stretch.
- Inhale through the centre and exhale into the twist.

20. Prone Kicks

Ten on each side

Mobilises the knee joints.
Warms the hamstrings.
Stretches the front of the thighs dynamically.

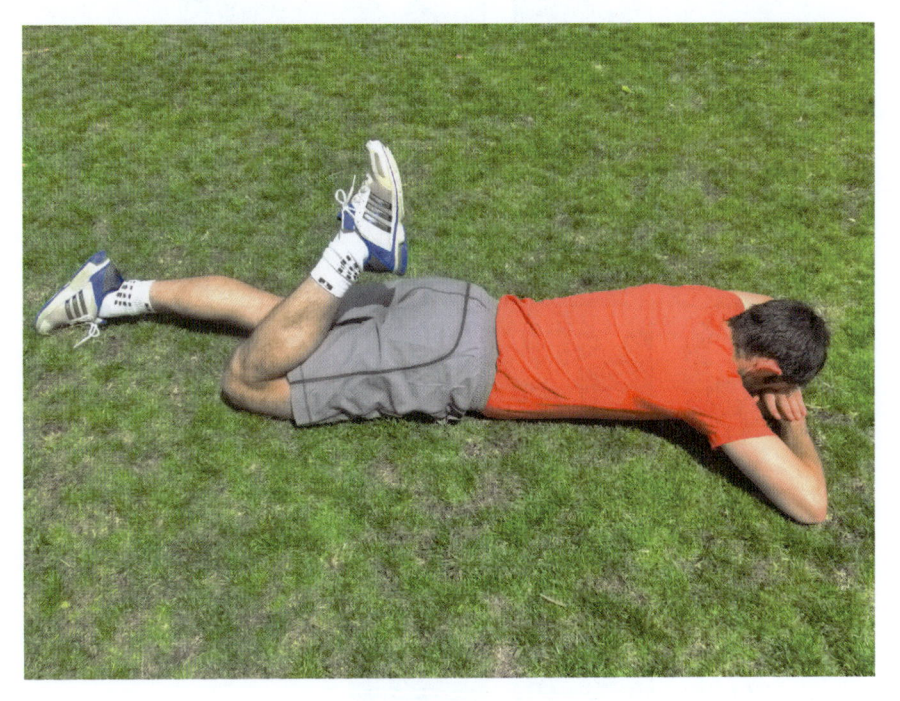

20: Prone Kicks

- Lie face down with your hands under your forehead.
- Keep your core muscles tight, flex your feet and alternate moving your heels towards your hips to activate your hamstrings and stretch your quadriceps.
- Breathe in as you move one leg and breathe out as you move the other leg.

21. Child's Pose

Hold for five seconds

Releases the lower back, hips, knees and ankles.

21: Child's Pose

- Come onto your hands and knees.
- Place your big toes together and your knees out wider than your hips.
- Sit your hips back on your heels until you feel a stretch in your groin muscles. Then stretch your arms forward and rest your forehead on the ground.

At the end of your program, slowly make your way back to a standing position and you're ready to continue with the rest of your warm-up.

Warm-Up

CHAPTER 3

Cool-down Stretches

When you've finished training, it is important to relax so that your body can begin the process of recovery. Once you've completed your cool-down, add these poses to release and stretch tight muscles and connective tissue in your legs, hips and back; restore joint movement; increase circulation and oxygen levels to your cells; calm your nervous system and return your body to its natural resting state.

This routine will take you 10 to 15 minutes, depending on how long you hold each pose. Aim to hold each stretch for a minimum of one minute and up to three minutes where possible. The longer you hold, the more you work on maintaining your flexibility and relaxing your body for rejuvenation.

TIPS FOR COOL-DOWN STRETCHES

BREATHING

Inhale and exhale through your nose if possible. Take slower, deeper breaths to relax and calm your nervous system, release tension from your muscles and connective tissue and increase oxygen levels in your body. It's important to breathe steadily throughout the sequence as holding your breath will cause tension to build up in your body.

TIMING

Hold each pose for a minimum of one minute and up to three minutes where possible. Holding for a longer time will allow a deeper stretch of the muscles and connective tissue and be more effective in releasing tension from your mind and body, allowing the recovery process to begin.

INTENSITY

Begin each stretch at 60 to 70 per cent of intensity so that you can remain calm and relaxed in each pose. As your body releases, the intensity of the stretch will increase so it's important to start in a position that gives you a mild stretch. Move slowly into each posture as you exhale and allow your muscles to relax before going deeper. A moderate stretch held for a longer time while relaxing in the pose will be more effective for releasing tension from the body and maintaining joint health.

SAFETY

Focus your mind on the sensations in your muscles and remain relaxed with your breathing. Maintain good posture and engage your core muscles by slightly pulling in the point just below your belly button. Come out of each pose slowly before moving into the next position. Respect your body. Never force yourself into a position you are not ready for and never over-stretch a muscle or joint. If any stretch causes you pain (not stretching discomfort), avoid that movement for the time being and seek advice from a qualified practitioner if necessary. Seek medical clearance prior to stretching if you have an injury. If your muscles are sore, stretch gently.

COOL-DOWN

1. Child's Pose

Hold for at least one minute
Calms the nervous system.
Gently stretches the lower back and groin muscles.
Releases the knees and fronts of the ankles and feet.

1: Child's Pose

- Come onto your hands and knees.
- Place your big toes together and your knees apart.
- Sit your hips back towards your heels. You will notice some compression on your hip, knee and ankle joints. Adjust your hips forward to reduce the pressure on your hips, knees or ankles if required.

- Rest your forehead on the ground and your arms beside your body, or reach your arms out in front of you to add a stretch to your shoulders.
- Hold for one to three minutes, taking deep breaths into your abdomen and focusing on sinking your hips to your heels with each exhale.
- If you have a knee or ankle injury, avoid this pose. (You can lie on your back with the soles of your feet together and your knees wide).

2. Toe Squat

Hold for one minute

Stretches the fascia underneath the feet.
Opens the toes.
Releases the Achilles tendons.

2: Toe Squat

- From a kneeling position, place your feet together, tuck all of your toes forward and rest on the balls of your feet.
- Sit your weight back towards your heels. This is an intense stretch for your feet and toes, so adjust your body weight forward if required.
- If your knees or toes are extremely tight, hold for a few breaths at a time and release in between.
- Maintain slow, deep breathing as you focus on relaxing your feet.
- This stretch is most effective without shoes.

3. Downward-Facing Dog

Hold for one minute

Calms the nervous system.
Stretches the calf muscles, the arches of the feet, hamstrings and gluteal muscles.
Stretches muscles between the ribs.
Increases blood flow to the lungs and oxygen levels in the body.

3a: Downward-Facing Dog   3b: Calf Stretch

- Place your hands shoulder-width apart on the ground and press your palms flat.
- Step your feet back as far as you can, turn them parallel and press your heels towards the ground, although they may not touch.
- Bend your knees, pull your ribcage in and lift your hips to the sky.
- Keep pressing firmly into your palms, draw the bottom tips of your shoulder blades into your back and breathe into the sides of your ribcage.
- To deepen your calf stretch, walk one heel at a time down towards the ground as you exhale, and hold for another 30 seconds each side.

4. Seal

Hold for 30 seconds to one minute

Extends the spine.
Stretches the abdominals.

4: Seal

- From Downward-Facing Dog, lower your body to the ground.
- Place your hands slightly forward and a bit wider than your shoulders, roll your shoulders back and straighten your arms to Seal. There should be a comfortable level of compression in your lower back and a stretch through your abdominal wall.
- If your back is tight, place your forearms on the ground with your elbows slightly forward of your shoulders for Sphinx.
- Keep your core muscles gently engaged and draw the bottom tips of your shoulder blades into your back to broaden your chest.
- Breathe into the front and sides of your ribcage.

5. Downward-Facing Dog

Hold for one minute

Opens the spine after the backbend.
Stretches the calf muscles, the arches of the feet, hamstrings and gluteal muscles.
Expands the ribcage.
Increases blood flow to the lungs and oxygen levels in the body.

5: Downward-Facing Dog

- Place your hands on the ground beside your ribcage, pull your abdominals in and press your hips up as high as you can.
- Turn your feet so they are parallel and lower your heels towards the ground. The stretch in your calf muscles and hamstrings will be less intense the second time around.
- Press firmly into your palms, draw the bottom tips of your shoulder blades into your back and breathe into the sides of your ribcage.

6. Dragon with Quad Stretch

Hold each pose for a minimum of one minute
Stretches the hip flexors and quadricep muscles of the back leg. Stretches the gluteal muscles of the front leg.

6a: Dragon

- From Downward-Facing Dog, step one foot forward between your hands.
- Drop your back knee to the ground.
- Sink your hips low, lift your chest and place your hands on your front thigh for Dragon (6a).

- Keep your core muscles engaged to assist the stretch in the front of your back hip.
- To increase the stretch around your hip muscles, raise the same arm as your back leg and reach it overhead with a slight side bend through your torso (6b).

6b: Dragon with Side Bend

- If you have the flexibility, reach around and hold your back foot with the same hand for Dragon with Quad Stretch (6c). For a stronger stretch in your thigh hold your ankle and flex your foot.

6c: Dragon with Quad Stretch

- Draw your foot towards the back of your hip to increase your thigh stretch. Slide your leg further back to avoid resting on your kneecap.
- Breathe steadily as you hold.
- If you can't reach your back foot, lie face down to hold one foot in a Lying Quad Stretch. As you hold your foot, press the front of your hip into the ground and draw your heel towards your buttock until you feel your thigh muscles stretch.

7. Swan

Hold for one to three minutes

Opens the hips.
Stretches the gluteal and groin muscles of the front leg.
Stretches the hip flexor muscles of the back leg.

7a: Swan

- From Dragon, walk your right foot across towards your left hand and lower your knee towards the ground behind your right hand (7a).
- Pull your front toes towards your shin and press the outside edge of your foot down to support your knee joint.
- If your gluteal muscles are tight your knee may not reach the ground and you can hold yourself here, or slide your front foot back slightly so you can rest over your front leg.
- If you're comfortable, slide your back knee further back and sink your hips low to increase the stretch in your gluteal, groin and hip flexor muscles.

- Focus on your exhale breath to deepen the stretch.
- If there is any discomfort in your front knee choose Deer (7b) instead.

7b: Deer

- In a seated position, place one leg across in front of you with a 90 degree bend in your knee. Flex your toes back towards your shin and press the outside edge of your foot down to support your knee joint.
- Place your other leg beside you with a 90 degree bend in your knee joint. Flex or point your foot depending on which position feels more comfortable on your knee.
- Inhale to straighten your back and as you exhale fold forward until you feel a stretch in the gluteal muscles of your front leg. You may also feel a stretch in the groin muscles of your back leg.
- Continue to breathe steadily as you hold.

8. Caterpillar

Hold for one to three minutes

Stretches the lower back, hamstrings and calf muscles. Releases the upper back and neck.

8a: Caterpillar

- Stretch both legs out in front of you, place your hands on your shins or the floor beside you, draw your abdominal muscles in and fold your torso over your legs as you exhale.
- Tilt your pelvis forward as you fold, then let your spine round as you relax into the pose. Drop your head towards your knees to release your upper spine and neck.
- Breathe slowly and deeply and relax.
- To release from the pose walk your hands back to lift your torso upright, then arch your back gently.

- If your hamstrings are extremely tight, or you have a disc injury to your spine choose Half Butterfly instead.

8b: Half Butterfly

- In a seated position, bend one knee and place your foot to your inner thigh. Straighten the other leg out slightly to the side.
- Engage your core muscles and fold forward as you exhale. Rest your hands on the ground once you feel the stretch in your groin and hamstrings.
- Bend your knee if your hamstrings are tight to allow a better stretch.
- Drop your chin towards your chest to stretch the back of your neck.
- Pull your front toes towards your shin to increase the stretch in your calf muscles.
- After completing both sides sit with your knees bent to 90 degrees and roll your legs slowly from side to side.

9. Dragonfly

Hold for three minutes

Stretches the long muscles of the groin and inner hamstrings. Releases the hips.

9: Dragonfly

- Slide your legs out as wide as you can and flex your toes to the sky.
- Place your hands behind your hips and straighten your spine. Bend your knees slightly if your hamstrings are tight.
- Relax your torso forward gently each time you exhale. If you are more flexible place your hands inside your thighs and walk them forward.
- Breathe slowly and deeply.
- To release from the pose draw your knees back together and hug them towards your chest for a few breaths.

10. Frog

Hold for one to three minutes

Stretches the short groin muscles.
Releases the hips.

10a: Frog

10b: Half Frog

- Come onto your hands and knees.
- Slide your knees as far apart as they will go, keeping them in line with your hips (10a).
- Slide your feet out as wide as your knees and draw your toes towards your shins. This will increase the stretch on your groin muscles.
- If your groin muscles are extremely tight and there is pressure on the insides of your knees use Half Frog (10b) with your big toes together.
- Rest on your forearms.
- Keep your abdominals pulled in (to maintain and support neutral spine).
- Breathe deeply and relax. Your knees will slide further apart as your groin muscles release.
- To come out of the pose, slide yourself forward or backward and lie on your back with your knees together.

11. Lying Hip Roll – feet wide

Hold for a minimum of one minute each side
Stretches the internal and external rotator muscles of the hip joints. Releases the rotator muscles of the spine.

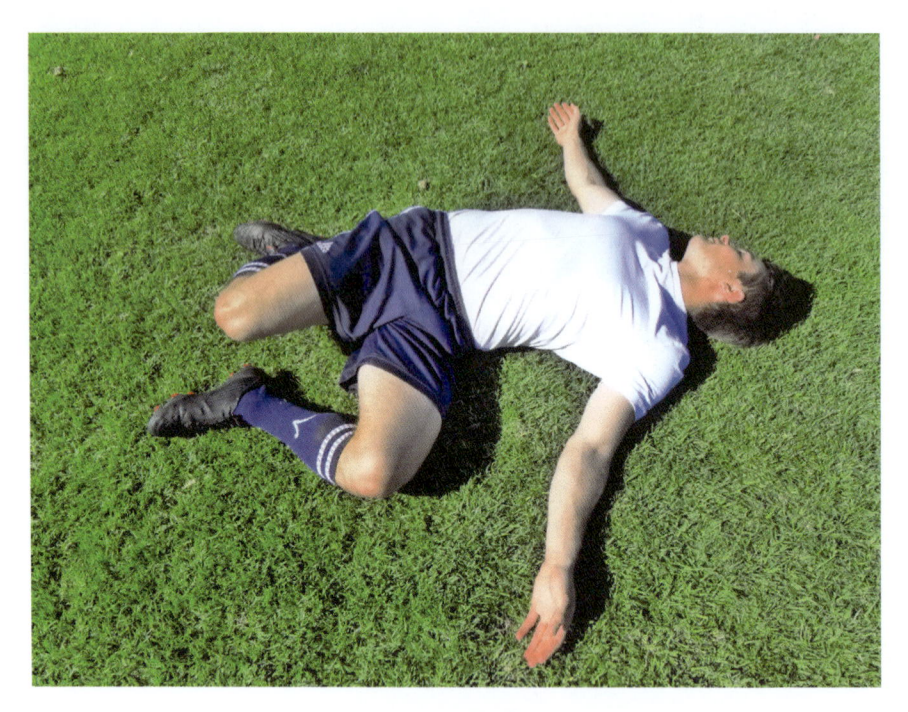

11: Lying Hip Roll – feet wide

- Lie on your back and bend your knees to 90 degrees.
- Position your feet wider than your hips.
- Drop your knees to one side, as close to the ground as you can, keeping the back of your shoulders down to deepen the stretch in your hip joints and lower torso.
- Breathe slowly and deeply.

12. Banana

Hold for a minimum of one minute each side

Stretches the entire side of the body, including the outer thigh (IT band), hip, lateral abdominals and breathing muscles between the ribs.

12: Banana

- Lie flat on your back with your legs together.
- Raise your arms overhead.
- Keep the back of your shoulders and hips on the ground and walk your arms and legs over to the right side.
- When you feel a stretch down the left side of your body, stop, hold the position and breathe deeply.
- Repeat on the other side.

13. Reclining Twist

Hold for one to three minutes each side
Releases tension from the muscles around the hips and spine.

13a: Reclining Twist

13b: Reclining Twist

- Lie on your back and bend your knees to 90 degrees.
- Cross your right leg over your left.
- Roll your knees to the left side (13a) and turn your head to the right. You may feel the stretch in your gluteal and neck muscles as well as your torso.
- Take slow deep breaths as you relax here.
- With your legs still crossed roll your knees to the right side (13b), turn your head to the left. You will notice the stretch move to the front of your other hip.
- Uncross your legs and roll back to the centre.
- Repeat with your left leg crossed over your right.
- When you've completed both sides again, extend your legs out and relax for a couple of breaths.

To complete your stretching routine, hug both knees into your chest and slowly roll to sitting before making your way back to standing.

Cool-down Stretches

These warm-up and cool-down sequences provide you with a basic introduction to using yoga with your football training program. With regular use, your body will begin to feel free as your mobility improves and your aches and pains should disappear sooner as your body recovers better. You can use the warm-up daily as part of your morning routine or the cool-down stretches at night to relax your mind and body at the end of each day. And once you learn the poses, you will be able to follow the sequence sheets easily.

I hope you enjoy the yoga advantage in your daily life as well as your training and playing!

NAMASTE.

ABOUT THE AUTHOR

Author of *The Yoga Edge: Techniques to Maximize Your Soccer Game*, Fiona holds a Master's Degree in Sports Science and is a Certified yoga teacher. She has been working with professional football players in the A-League in Australia since 2008, assisting them with body maintenance to reduce injury rates and enhance their football performance on the pitch. She has been the yoga teacher for Sydney Football Club for a number of seasons, conducting weekly yoga sessions and guiding players with their yoga warm-up and cool-down routines.

ABOUT THE MODELS

TERRY MCFLYNN

Terry McFlynn is a professional footballer from Northern Ireland. He began his career at Queens Park Rangers Football Club in the English Premier League and then played for various teams in England before moving to Sydney Football Club in the A-League in Australia. Terry has played for Sydney FC for nine years and is the only remaining foundation player at any club in the A-League. He has won two Championships and one Premiership during his nine-year tenure. He captained the club for four years prior to passing the captaincy on to the great Alessandro Del Piero. He also played for, and captained, his country at every age level from Under 15 to Under 23.

Terry holds a Master's Degree in Coach Education from Sydney University and will continue to apply his professional and academic knowledge in the sporting arena in future years.

JOEL HARDWICK

Australian football player Joel Hardwick has played for the Newcastle Jets youth team and National Premier League sides Central Coast Mariners Academy and Blacktown City Football Club.

Watch Joel play on http://vimeo.com/78887195